642

THINGS ABOUT YOU
(THAT I LOVE)

BY THE SAN FRANCISCO
WRITERS' GROTTO
INTRODUCTION BY JASON ROBERTS

D1384375

CHRONICLE BOOKS
SAN FRANCISCO

EDITOR

Jason Roberts

CONTRIBUTORS

Natalie Baszile	David Munro
Elizabeth Bernstein	Louise Nayer
E. B. Boyd	Bridget Quinn
Xandra Castleton	Jason Roberts
Jane Ciabattari	Ethel Rohan
Laurie Ann Doyle	Julia Scott
Alastair Gee	Maw Win
Anisse Gross	Andy Wright
Mary Ladd	

ISBN: 978-1-4521-5839-6

Manufactured in China

Designed by Michael Morris

10 9 8 7 6

Chronicle Books
680 Second Street
San Francisco, California 94107
www.chroniclebooks.com

Chronicle books and gifts are available at special quantity discounts to corporations, professional associations, literacy programs, and other organizations. For details and discount information, please contact our premiums department at corporatesales@chroniclebooks.com or at 1-800-759-0190.

How do I love thee? Let me count the ways . . .

In her famous *Sonnets from the Portuguese*, the poet Elizabeth Barrett Browning counted only seven. Here at the San Francisco Writers' Grotto, we couldn't help thinking there were more. At least 642, to be exact.

Here's a little book to inventory your big heart. Contemplating and completing these 642 entries will bring out both the lover and the writer in you, as you celebrate what makes a special someone so special. After adding your insights, you can offer this book *to* that special someone, as a unique keepsake. Explore, expound, share, and enjoy.

JASON ROBERTS
San Francisco Writers' Grotto

The way I realized I really liked you

The way I realized you liked me in return

If our relationship had a mascot, it would be

If our relationship had a theme song, it would be

If our relationship had a logo, it would be

If our relationship had a secret code name, it would be

If you could learn only
one dance, it would be

If you had to assume
another identity, you'd
probably pick
a name like

If you were on a game
show, I'd introduce
you as

If you inherited a farm,
you'd want to grow

The most thoughtful thing you've done,
without being asked

The gentlest way you told me something harsh

How you never push me to

How you *always* encourage me to

The cute nickname you call me in public

The other nickname you call me in private

The various terms of endearment you tried out
along the way

Three instances where you waited until the
time was right

Three and a half times you've changed my mind about
something (I'm still not fully convinced
about that last one)

If you got lost in a city, the first place I'd look
for you would be

If you got lost in the woods,
I'd find you doing this

If you got lost in a theme park,
I'd head straight to

What I'd give you if I won the lottery

If you won the lottery, you would

Our first inside joke—the one that was funny to
just the two of us

That time you persuaded me to let go of a grudge

My first impression of you

What I got wrong

What I got right

That ridiculous joke you told

That ridiculous joke you tried to tell,
but got the punchline all wrong

How you behaved when you first met one
of my friends

What you said when I first took you to
meet my parents

The thing you wear that brings out your eyes

The thing you wear that makes you look glamorous

The thing you wear when you want to be cozy

How I love to picture you: a portrait in words

If they made a movie out of our relationship, we would be played by

The movie would be called

Its tagline would be

The movie would be rated

The time you made me feel better without
saying a word

The three ways you give yourself permission to be vulnerable

How you act around children

How you act around old people

How you act around weird people

If I left you alone in a room with only pencils and
paper, after three hours you would have

The three values you clearly picked up
from your father

The three values of yours that your mother is
probably responsible for

If they turned our relationship into a book, you would find it in this section of the bookstore

Here are the names of the first seven chapters of the book

It's probably better if we leave this chapter out of the book

The thing you insist on doing, despite all logic

What you're going to keep doing, despite the odds

What you whisper in my ear to wake me gently

What you whisper in my ear when I'm
having a nightmare

What you whisper in my ear when I'm snoring and
you want me to roll over

If you had lived a hundred years earlier, this is
what you'd do as a profession:

How I know you're really paying attention

How I know you're zoning out

The thing I miss most when we're apart

The thing I'm surprised I miss when we're apart

The thing I always do when we're apart

How you patiently listen to

How you want me to patiently listen to

How you are not interested in hearing about

Something you've memorized

How you never complain about

How you managed to stay calm when

How you never give up when it comes to

How you forgave me for

What you're always losing

What you'll never lose

The three ways you show your loyalty to friends

That if you started
doing this,
you'd never stop

What you're like when
you're tipsy

Your favorite song to
sing in the shower

The most absentminded
thing you do

My silly habit that you mock but secretly love

How I feel waking up next to you

My favorite story about you as a kid

That you remembered that I

The four things I know you'll never do again

That the most peaceful I've ever seen you was when

How you are an expert on

How you are clueless about

How you want to learn more about

Your snappiest comeback

Your snappiest comeback that came too late
(but that you shared with me anyway)

Your nicest insincerity

Your most impressive rationalization

If I suspected you'd been replaced by a robot,
here's how I would test to prove it was you:

That I'll never find this in your refrigerator

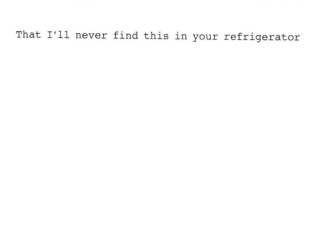

That your fridge never seems to lack

The three things I know you'd change about
yourself, if you could

The three things I know you'd change about me
(but would never mention)

If you could pick only one deadly sin to indulge in,
it would be

If you could pick only one deadly sin to condemn,
it would be

A description of the object you're most like

A forecast of the weather you're most like

A guidebook's description of the place
you're most like

An ode to the things that make you you

Your favorite tree to
sit under

That you still
believe in

What I find on your
face sometimes

How you air-guitar

That one occasion when you refused to let someone
put you in your place

The four things you always do in the snow

The two things you always do in the rain

The seven things you always do in the sun

These three things I know you take satisfaction in:

The liner notes I'd write for an album about you

Lines from a rap song I'd write for you

I got freewheelin' and wrote a Bob Dylan
song for you:

I can connect your freckles to make a
constellation! Which I'll call

How you've tolerated my
sudden enthusiasms, including

How I know you're
keeping a secret

How you turn a
blind eye to

How I can't stay mad at
you when you

How you crinkle your nose
when

These three things you're naturally gifted at

This one seemingly effortless skill you worked
hard to achieve

The way you show determination

The way you show gratitude

The way you show enthusiasm

How, when you smile, your eyes

How people are always telling me that you

How smart you are about

What you always have time for

What you'll never have time for

The thing you said to me once, and will never need to say again

The three things you say that I hope you'll keep saying

If you'd met me when we were both five years old,
you'd have probably

The words you use when you want to swear, but can't

The wardrobe item you own in overabundance

The thing you do before you let go of my hand

The thing you do for me, because I can't

The thing you do for me, because I won't

The three ways in which you're still a child

The three ways in which you're wise
beyond your years

A speculative description of our life together on our very own planet

How you're willing to be the strong one when

How you let me be the strong one when

If you packed me a lunch designed to make me
lonesome for you, it would contain

That I know I could leave these three things
in your care

The historical figure you could probably best
impersonate is

The foreign language I can most easily imagine you
speaking is _____ because

The simplest possible caricature of you would
contain only

The one thing you can't stand losing at

The time you let me win

How when I saw your house for the first time,
I thought

How when you saw my house for the first time,
I thought

The first time I wanted to tell you something and I was afraid of how you'd react

How you reacted

What you could be cynical about, but aren't

The thing you conceal from me
(but really don't need to)

What you're uncomfortable discussing
(but do anyway)

When I knew I had gotten you the perfect gift

When you gave me the perfect gift

The four ways in which I prefer your judgment and taste to mine

---

The thing you let me think I'm getting away with

The thing I didn't know about myself, until you
pointed it out to me

How, when you want me to stop taking myself
too seriously, you

That choice you made for me, when I couldn't

The six words I can't imagine coming
out of your mouth

If you filled in for the Cheshire Cat, the last part
of you to disappear would be

The thing you always do with more style than is
strictly necessary

If we fused together into one person,
that person would

The three ways you show
your smarts

The emoji that's most
characteristic of you

That thing you know how
to do, but I don't

That time you read
my mind

If you were head of a network, here are the shows
you'd bring back (and how you'd improve them)

If you had exactly five minutes to make me
feel better, you'd

The two things about me that nobody knows but you

The two things about you that nobody knows but me

That nice thing that you do begrudgingly,
but do nonetheless

The thing you do openly that I'm still a little
shocked about

The thing you know quite well, but probably couldn't
explain if your life depended upon it

How at first I thought
you were kidding when

How you gently tease
me about

How you flirt
with me, still

How much you enjoy

The time I got bad news, and you

The time I got fantastic news, and you

A colorful confession of the things about us we
wouldn't want anyone else to know

The best way you ever made it up to me

That time that we got lost, looking for

The place where we ended up

That when you have to pick a number,
the number is usually

What you would eat all the time (if you could)

The color that suits you best

The three ordinary objects that you're
sentimentally attached to, and the reasons why

The way you let me

The way you don't let me

The time when I missed you the most was

I was especially grateful you were there when

Where we went on our fourth date

The first thing I learned about you
that surprised me

This is how I would describe the way you and I fight

I never would have crossed your path if I hadn't

And we never would have gotten together
if you hadn't

These four ways in which you are
(gloriously) contradictory

The animal you remind
me of when you dance

That when you dance
you always

Your go-to karaoke song

The ways I'd spot you
in a crowd

The reason I'm convinced
we met in a past life

You had me at

What only you
can pull off

How quickly you
smile when I

That time I witnessed you being brutally
honest with yourself

The five things about you that I wish would rub off on me

Your sense of humor, in three words

Your value system, in three words

The dish you can cook that I didn't even know
existed before I met you

The dish you learned to cook, just for me

How I can tell when you're getting hungry

If they ever erect a statue in your honor,
you'll be holding

That your favorite part
of any parade is

Our seven favorite
neighborhood haunts

Your favorite
childhood book

Your favorite things to
do on a ferry ride

A list of words I'm fairly certain you've made up

I've invented a new word to describe you. It's

What you showed me about the night sky

That trick for cleaning that I never knew about

If I want to get you out of a funk in a hurry,
all I have to do is

The random things that
make you yell at the TV

That food you always eat
off my plate

Your rituals, such as

Your hands, because

How you acted, that time I was least myself

If they named a diet after your eating habits,
it would be called

That trick you have to push me outside of my
comfort zone

The ways you make me feel better after I really
embarrass myself

The three things you think are great about me that
most people miss

I'll never get enough of
your

How when you walk,
you look like

That even when we're
old, I know you'll still

How I knew you
were a keeper

If you didn't want me to miss you too much when
you're gone, you'd invent a machine that

The time when I saw you act the most loyal

That time when I was proud to know you

How I know you like what I'm wearing

That you'd like it if I styled my hair so that

Matching tattoos? You'd probably suggest

That your style of procrastination is

What I know you indulge in when I'm gone for a while

The chore you secretly enjoy doing

The time when I saw you the most scared

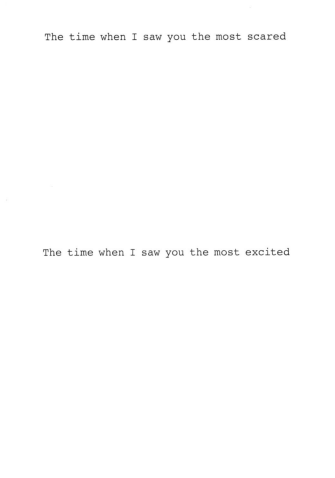

The time when I saw you the most excited

How passionately you feel about

How you refuse to be embarrassed by

How you've never been afraid to try

These six foods I never would have tried
if I hadn't met you

These five places you showed me, where I'd never
been before

These three things you guessed right about me when we first met

The time I fell asleep, and you

If you overheard someone badmouthing me, you
wouldn't hesitate to

The very first thing you gave me

That time when you were foolish on purpose

The way you helped me say good-bye to

That time you unclogged the toilet at

How you negotiated a great price for

You were born in the wrong era. You really belong in
the _____ century, because

The most endearing way you've said good-bye
to me was when

The names we always joke
we'd give to our kids

Your coolest
party trick

What you scrawl in the
margins of books

The bands we most
disagree on

The incredibly weird thing that you like to eat

The very normal food that you think is gross

How you generously pretend you've forgotten
the time when

The secret nickname we
have for your mother

How you feel about
friendship

The four things you're
falsely modest about

The empathy you
show for

If we spent a day together without exchanging a
single word, you'd

The time you tricked me (I forgive you!)

If you joined the dark side, you'd really enjoy

If you joined the circus, your act would be called

What kind of cookie you are

Your geekiest quality

If I painted your portrait, here's how I'd pose you

The good habit I have because of you

Your "bad" habit (that I'll never try to change)

The one thing you always do before
leaving the house

The book I never would have read if you hadn't
suggested it

The movie you dragged me to that was actually
really good

The funniest thing you've ever said
in your sleep

The most enigmatic thing you've ever said
in your sleep

How you've never been a
snob about

How handy you are at

How you make me laugh

How you taught me to

The first time I knew you loved me, even though you
hadn't said it yet

How I know other people
find you attractive

How when I'm cold at
night in bed, you

How when we cook
together, you

How you look at me from
across the table

The first time I was nervous around you
(and this is why)

My favorite souvenir from our early dates

And why I kept it

What I didn't know I was compromising on,
before I met you

Your zero tolerance policy on

The reason I feel safe telling you how I feel

The ways you disagree without being disagreeable

The most subtle jab I've heard you utter

The things you put up with from my family,
in order to make me happy

What you would wear if we went to the opera

What you would order in a Michelin-starred
restaurant

A tribute to your most treasured object

Looking back, this is the thing I'll wish I did more
of with you

And this is the thing I'll wish we'd done less

How when I stub
my toe, you

The sound you make
when you

Your secret talent

How it feels when you
touch me

That time when I acted kind of badly and you were
nice about it

The things you show up for, even though I know
you're not really interested

The thing I used to want to change about you
(but now I realize it's one of your best qualities)

The thing you do that I wish I could do as well

Your spirit animal

The reason your spirit animal is a good match for
my spirit animal

Based on everything you've told me about your
childhood, I would describe it as

That old photo of you that I love, and you hate

The three things you do that remind me where
you grew up

The joke of yours I've stolen and told
to other people

The first time I had a problem and you treated it
like it was your problem, too

....

....

....

....

....

....

....

....

....

....

....

....

The time we went hiking and you

The time we went skiing and you

The TV show you're most addicted to, and what that reveals about you

How you always sing along to

How you're obsessed with

The first time I felt lucky to be with you

The thing we like to do together that no one knows about

Your real life
superhero quality

This is what I believe
about you

How we're alike

How you worked so hard to

The thing you leave around the house that makes me think of you

That if there was a fire, the first thing you'd grab (after me) would be

What I find in your pockets

How your best impression is of

How your worst impression is of

How when you sing in the car, you

How when you eat sushi, you

How when you kiss me, you

The last time something happened and I couldn't
wait to tell you about it

If I had met you three and a half years earlier
than I did, I probably would have

That thing you do when you're mad, but don't
want to admit it

How I know when you're thinking something,
but it's too mean to say

How you get when you're embarrassed

That your go-to recipe is

That your go-to drink is

That story you always forget that you
already told me

The person you love the most (after me)

The person you miss the most

The first time I felt safe because you were there

The strangest dream I've ever had about you

The things you've brought me back from your travels

In praise of the things you notice

If your clothes could talk, here's what
they'd say about you

If we're ever stranded on a desert island together,
the three things that we'd better have with us are

How we have that song and what it means to us

If love is a drug, then you're my

It wasn't your smile I noticed first. It was

The five things you own that say the most about who you are

What you wanted to be when you grew up

What you still want to be when you grow up

A history of the places you've taken me

Did you know you have a catchphrase? It's

The foods you make me hungry for

The five silly emojis you like to use

Your three favorite things to tell me
about your workday

The three things you do when watching sports

The three things you need when we are in the car

That you like the smell of

That you can't stand the smell of

How I discovered your sentimental side

That time you bought a fancy bottle to celebrate

That time you had an impromptu music jam because

That time you decorated for

If we woke up to find ourselves with superpowers,
they'd be

If our relationship had a motto it would be

The first New Year's resolution we made as a couple

How you make a trip to the grocery store
into an adventure

How I know you're a bigger romantic than I am

The *Star Wars* character you most remind me of

That time your Halloween costume was

The Jane Austen character you most remind me of

That thing you wear that drives me crazy—
in a good way

That thing you wear that drives me crazy—
in an it's-making-me-crazy way

The classic movie star you're most like

The current movie star you're most like

The reason you believe in second (and third) chances for your friends

---

The thing you do when you concentrate, that you're
not aware you're doing

That one thing you refuse to throw out, sell, or
give away because you're going to *use* it some day

These two things I thought were goofy about you
when we met (that I now find endearing)

If you wanted to genuinely scare me,
all you'd have to do is

If I said, "Let's go get into trouble,"
you'd take that to mean

If you didn't want me to eat something,
you'd cover it in

Your culinary obsessions
(listed in reverse chronological order)

That I could make you *really* cranky by taking away
this one item

The thing I know you do just to get along
with your coworkers

What you ask permission for, even though
you don't need to

Your most embarrassing story

The story you love to exaggerate
(and how you improve it)

How, if you don't have a bookmark, you keep your place in a book with

The article of clothing that always makes me think of you

The impractical pet you want, but will probably never get

The reason my friends are happy that we're together

The three words I would use to describe your face

The way you react when one of your favorite songs
comes on the radio

That time you surprised my whole family by

The way you let me have the last

That time you gave me the first taste of

The thing I know you're right about
(but I just can't admit it)

The two things you do that make me say
"You're a dork" (in a good way)

The three things you do when you think
I'm not looking

If a butterfly flaps its wings in California, it might cause a hurricane in Florida. These are the ways in which the world has changed as a result of our getting together:

_____

_____

_____

_____

_____

_____

_____

_____

_____

_____

The five ways you show you care when I'm sick

The five things you need when you're sick

The three ways you like to spend your "me time"

The three ways you give me "me time"

How you give me tissues when I cry at

How you cry at

Quixotic. Narcissistic. Herculean. Here's an
adjective named after you, its meaning,
and its use in a sentence:

The three things you persuaded me to try
(and I'm glad I did)

The items of my clothing you've commandeered

The thing I love about you that I hate
in other people

That when we met, I never would have
guessed that you

The most unexpected compliment you ever gave me

What I told my friends after our first date

Three of your facial expressions that
only I understand

The kind of face you make when you're frustrated

The way your inner child comes out when you

The flirty cues you give me from across the room

Those four things you do in front of me that I *know* you'd never do in front of anyone else

A tale of you, me, and that swimming pool

The three things you do when playing your
favorite board game

The three things you do when playing your
favorite video game

Your four favorite things in a convenience store

Your three favorite things to eat when you
have the munchies

The two things you always do on
your morning commute

The best books you've brought into my life

How you get nervous talking about money because

How you hate the sound of

How you slow down whenever you see

The funny sayings you use
(that I totally use now, too)

If I could go back in time I'd want to be
there when you

The way you are always cordial to the friend of
mine whom I know you like the least

That gift that seemed practical,
but was really quite romantic

One way you've shown me you're unlike anyone
else I've loved

That you remember where you were when you heard
the news that

How when you've got something important to do, you
always wear your "good luck _____ "

The time of day when you always reach for my hand

The most surprising things in your suitcase on our first weekend away together

The conversation you have with me when we can't sleep

You tell everyone your favorite movie
is _____, but I know it's really

The bad habit we both have, but that's so fun
it's worth it

That you like to research info
about _____ online

That question I know you'd like to ask me
(but haven't yet)

Your most endearing humblebrag

You'd never guess it, but I really like the way you

Your endearing childhood memory

That in high school you were known for

That in college you were known for

What I buy a lot more of, now that you're in my life

What you're still grieving, after all these years

What you say instead of "I told you so"

The times you went out
of your way to

When you appeared in a
dream of mine, and told me

When we took a class
together and you

That time we snuck into

The quality of your laughter,
which is best described as

If there were a mountain named after you,
it would be called

Five things that are the same color as your hair

The way you bite your lip when

The way you bite my lip when

That time you visited my hometown with me, and we

Our proverbial "across the room" moment

When we stood in my childhood bedroom and you

How, when I'm exhausted after a long day, you

How knowing you has made me stop regretting

How I know it's time to stop talking when you

The way you close your eyes when

The way you open your eyes wide when

The time you tried to be sexy
(and how you recovered when it didn't work out)

The time you tried to be sexy (and succeeded)

That the main reason you stop reading a book is

That no one else truly appreciates my

That when you sing, it sounds like

The first thing you do in the morning

The last thing you do before you go to bed

What you pay attention to when you're outside

What you pay attention to when you're inside

My memories of the loudest you've ever been

My memories of the smelliest you've ever been

That if I hadn't met you, I would never have

The most public place in which you've kissed me

The feeling I get from watching you breathe

The promise you made me years ago, and kept

The sweetest text you ever sent me

The dirtiest you ever got with me
(you know, like in the mud)

A chronicling of the craziest thing
we've ever done together

A chronicling of the funniest time
we've ever had together

That time you bought me designer _____ because

That time you wore designer _____ because

The gadget you love to use that drives me crazy

The direction you like the toilet paper to go

The celebrity crush you've forgiven me for

That your favorite thing about your hometown is

That I never thought I'd fall for someone who

That your teachers thought you would become

That you have pictures of _____ on your phone

That you have pictures of _____ on your desk

That in your family you're known for

That at work you're known for

When we saw our image together in the
mirror and you

The first time I heard your laugh across the room

How you charmed my mother the day you met her

That you'd rather be a _____ than a

That you'd rather visit _____ than

Until I met you, I never knew anyone who collected

In the ice cream shop, I know you'll probably pick

What you would *definitely* do on a deserted island

That your favorite ways to save money are

That your favorite ways to spend money are

The things about you I don't ever want to change

What I'm going to love most about you as
we grow older

The song you play when you want to romance me

The most mortified I've ever been in front of you

Those three times you were epically spontaneous

The most amazing Scrabble word you ever
beat me with

The three household staples you always buy

The three household staples you always kinda forget

The funniest joke you ever told me

The dumbest joke you ever told me

If you were a plant,
you would be

If you were a color,
you would be

If our relationship were
a sport, it would be

If you became a
zombie, I'd

The latest we ever stayed up

The longest we ever stayed in bed

The most expensive thing we've ever done together

What we did when the electricity was off

The greatest party you've ever thrown

The antediluvian term of endearment
I call you without irony

The four ways you've made me a better person

The last time you touched me, for no reason at all

That word you always mispronounce
(and I promise to stop correcting you)

.

The word you think I pronounce funny
(but I swear I'm right)

The five ways you deal with boring car rides

The story you tell of how we met,
cocktail-party version

The things you leave out of that story

The three things you can't make up your mind about

How I can tell when you're stressing out

The way you know exactly what I want when

If our relationship were a mystery novel,
the title would be

If our relationship were a heavy metal band,
the band's name would be

If I were presenting you with an award for Best Partner in a Romantic Relationship, this is how I'd introduce you:

And this would be your acceptance speech:

How you saved our worst time together

How you made our best time together

Our best camping story

Our worst camping story

If you were a bottle of fine wine, you'd taste like

The appetizer most like you is

If bumper stickers were mandatory, yours would read

If you ran the world, everyone would be issued a
supply of

Your most eloquent silence was when

The note you left me, that time when

That amazing meal you made for me, when

The way you eat spaghetti

That on road trips
you always

That when you doodle
you always draw

The five things you like
to do at work

What you're like when
you're on a roll

What we said at 2 A.M.

What we would say to each other in outer space

The ways in which you use your imagination

Your energy when you talk about

In a vintage Hollywood romance, our characters'
names would be

A description of you on the menu of
a fancy restaurant

The nerdy way you invented of saying *I love you* when someone else is around

Your ingenious hack (that breached my firewall)

How I would describe you to someone who
had never met you

The first story about us

That thing I still can't believe we got away with

That time you bought my family dinner because

That time you fixed my _____ by

Your favorite cocktail

Your default dessert

What I would be doing right now if you and I had
never met

If we had met in second grade, I would have dreamed
this about our future

What you brought me instead of flowers

That time I was late to meet you and you

When I picked you up at the airport and you

How I can tell that you're tired, but don't want to
let it show

What you do with your hands when you're trying not
to fidget

If you had to be handcuffed to someone (who wasn't me!), you'd pick

You wouldn't mind being stranded in the rain with _____ because

I thought you actually liked _____ when we
first met, but I learned later that you were only
trying to impress me.

The outfit you were wearing when we first met

That your favorite sport is

That your favorite thing at the farmers market is

That your favorite cheap thrill is

The ways in which you're not just good to me, but
good *for* me

How I know I could do things, bad things, and you'd
still stand by me

That thing you thought was hysterically funny when no one else did

That time you wore comfy pants with me on the couch because

Our life together if we had lived
among the dinosaurs

How we would live together inside the
stomach of a whale

How you rescued me from a situation I couldn't get out of alone

One of your favorite
quotations

The tattoo on your

Eight things that are
the same color as
your eyes

Your biggest pet peeve

What you look like when you're sleeping

The way you got through Thanksgiving with my family
without offending anyone, despite

That when I got that awful haircut you said

The habit you gave up for me

That time you improvised a gift for

The two things you did to impress me during our first month together (but didn't have to, because I was already hooked)

That time you double-dared me to

The ways you make me
tingle

Your classiest move
ever

How I melt when you

Together we look like

The life and times of the best gift you ever gave me

The dream of yours you told me about, in which we

The way you remind me of
my favorite

How you're willing to
spend time with my

How quickly you bounce
back from

We're like an ecosystem
because

I designed a T-shirt about us, that only we'll get.
Here's a description:

The kindest thing you've ever done,
told in a one-act play

A prose poem detailing the traditions we've made
together

What I would write in a letter to get you excused
from jury duty

A State of the Union address about us